World War II Jeep

Written by David Doyle

In Action®

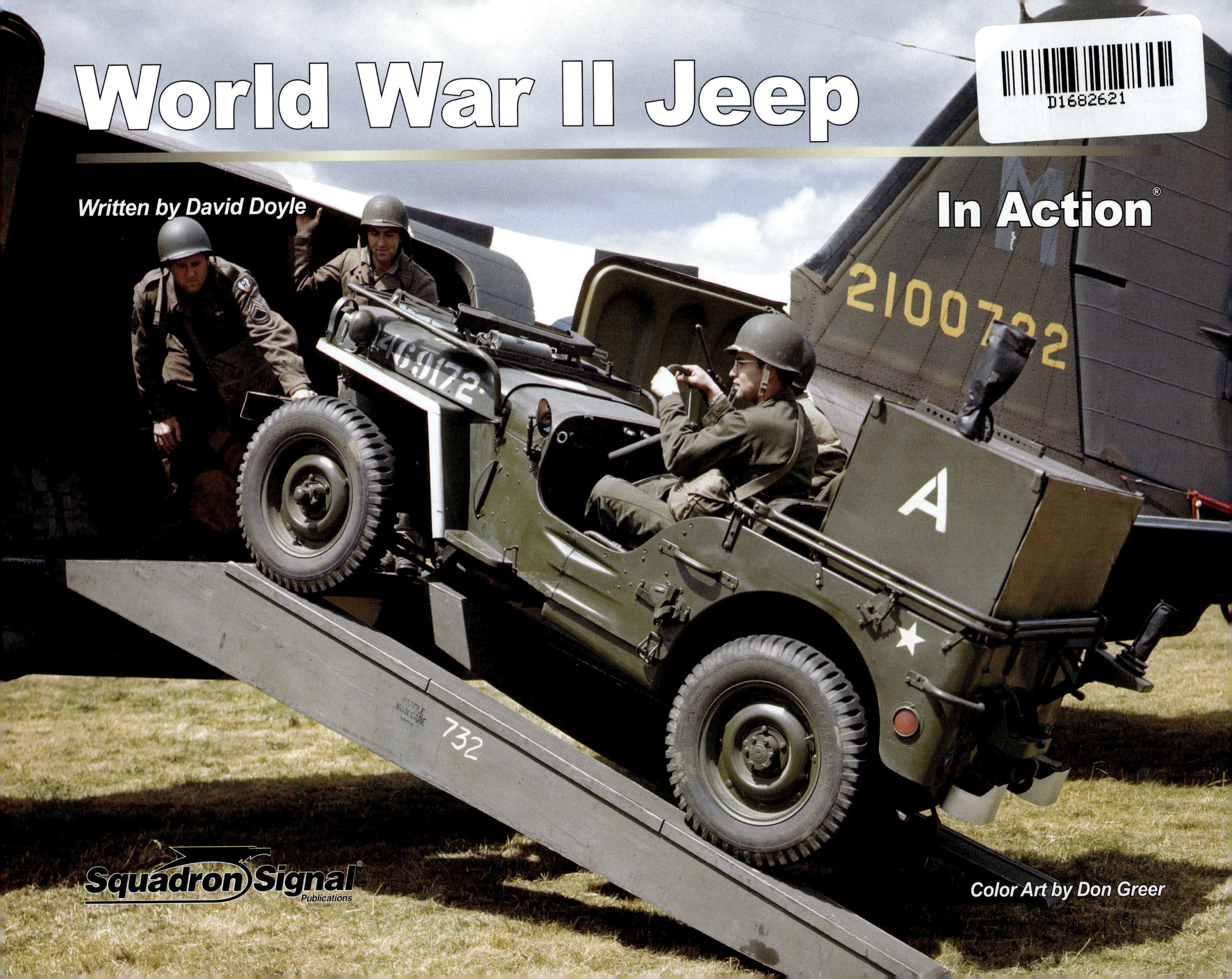

Squadron/Signal Publications®

Color Art by Don Greer

D1682621

(Front Cover) The U.S. military jeep has hundreds of uses. This Ford GPW served as a radio-communications vehicle for an artillery battalion's command post.

(Back Cover) U.S. troops riding in a Willys MB await instructions to advance during training maneuvers in World War II. On the bumper are markings for Troop B, 17th Cavalry Reconnaissance Squadron, XX Corps. Standing behind the jeep is a British motorcycle dispatch rider. (National Archives)

About the In Action® Series

In Action® books, despite the title of the genre, are books that trace the development of a single type of aircraft, armored vehicle, or ship from prototype to the final production variant. Experimental or "one-off" variants can also be included. Our first *In Action®* book was printed in 1971.

ISBN 978-0-89747-812-0
Proudly printed in the U.S.A.
Copyright 2016, 2009 Squadron/Signal Publications
1115 Crowley Drive, Carrollton, TX 75006-1312 U.S.A.

All rights reserved. No part of this publication may be reproduced, stored in a retrieval system, or transmitted in any form by means electrical, mechanical, or otherwise, without written permission of the publisher.

Military/Combat Photographs and Snapshots

If you have any photos of aircraft, armor, soldiers, or ships of any nation, particularly wartime snapshots, why not share them with us and help make Squadron/Signal's books all the more interesting and complete in the future? Any photograph sent to us will be copied and returned. Electronic images are preferred. The donor will be fully credited for any photos used. Please send them to:

Squadron/Signal Publications
1115 Crowley Drive
Carrollton, TX 75006-1312 U.S.A.
www.SquadronSignalPublications.com

(Title Page) A radio-equipped jeep is loaded in the cargo bay of a C-47 transport bound for France in 1944. The edge of the jeep's front fender is painted white, and the numerals of the registration number on the hood are in a nonstandard font. (National Archives)

Acknowledgments

Jeep is a registered trademark of Fiat Chrysler Automobiles. The author recognizes that some words, model names and designations, for example, mentioned herein are the property of the trademark holder. The author uses them for identification purposes only. This is not an official publication.

This book would not have been possible without the generous assistance of Tom Kailbourn, Scott Taylor, Jim Gilmore, Reg Hodgson, and Tom Wolboldt. In addition to these individuals, additional photos came from these sources: John McCleaf; Robert Notman; the Patton Museum; the Military History Institute; the National Archives; the Library of Congress; Army Motors, the United States Marine Corps; the United States Navy; the Ordnance Museum; the U.S. Army Engineer School History Office; and the Don F. Pratt Museum. I give a special thanks to my wife Denise, who – in addition to scanning innumerable photos – provided unflagging support.

Introduction

The World War II Jeep has attained an almost mythic status in popular culture. Over time, more than 640,000 of the rugged little trucks were built. Its status results from tales of returning servicemen and wartime propaganda from the U.S. War Department and Willys-Overland Motors.

While the Ordnance Department took over motor vehicle procurement for the US Army on 1 August 1942, prior to that date the responsible agency was the Quartermaster Corps. As the Ordnance Corps would be later, the Quartermaster Corps was tasked with economically and efficiently procuring vehicles that met the requirements of the branches of the Army.

During the 1930s, as clouds of war gathered in Europe and Asia, the U.S. Army wanted to replace the horse and mechanize cavalry scouts. Motorcycles initially found favor, but many in the Army regarded their lack of passenger and cargo-carrying capacity as a serious drawback.

By late 1938 the Secretary of War had endorsed the Quartermaster Corps Technical Committee plan to field ½-ton 4x4 trucks as a standard model, some with special bodies for command and reconnaissance.

In order to fulfill these desires, the Chief of Infantry established a requirement for a vehicle with a maximum weight of 750-1,000 pounds, maximum height of 36-inches, four-wheel drive, capability of mounting a .50-caliber machine gun, and off-road performance equal to that of the ½-ton vehicles, while laden with two men and 3,000 rounds of machine gun ammunition.

The Chief of Infantry desired that 40 such vehicles be procured for extended service testing, and so recommended to the Chief of Staff. The Chief of Cavalry concurred, requesting that his office be kept informed on this development, and further requesting 20 of the vehicles be assigned to Cavalry for testing.

As the vehicle was not armored, the Adjutant General's office (AG) sent the requirements to the Quartermaster General for a recommendation. Because of the purchase in 1938 of three lightweight chassis from the American Bantam Company, the Quartermaster General felt that firm may be a suitable source for such a vehicle.

The Ordnance Department, which previously had been involved in the testing of the lightweight Howie Machine Gun Carrier, was asked through its technical committee for recommendations as well. On 15 June 1940 the AG asked the Chief of Ordnance to consider the Bantam car, in view of the Ordnance, Cavalry and Infantry requirements.

An Ordnance sub-committee, along with representatives of the Quartermaster Corps, Cavalry and Infantry visited the Butler, Pennsylvania, plant of the American Bantam Company, reviewed the firm's products and facilities, and discussed the proposed new vehicle with representatives of the firm.

In June 1940 the subcommittee reported that the development of the new vehicle should be handled through the Quartermaster Corps, and that the new vehicle should be considered as a replacement for the motorcycle and sidecar.

The Secretary of War approved the subcommittee's recommendation, and approved the expenditure of not more than $175,000 of Quartermaster funds for the project, with the objective of obtaining 70 vehicles, which were to be available in late summer 1940. The Quartermaster Technical Committee met with Infantry and Cavalry representatives on 1 July and refined the specifications. These included a provision for eight of the vehicles to be equipped with four-wheel steer in addition to four-wheel drive. It was felt that four-wheel steer would enhance mobility.

Bid solicitations were sent to over 135 manufacturers. In response, bids for the initial production of the ¼-ton vehicles, both 2-wheel and 4-wheel steer, were received from American Bantam and Willys-Overland. On 25 July 1940 the contract for 70 of the new vehicles was awarded to American Bantam.

The promise held by the concept of these vehicles was such that on 18 October 1940 a further procurement of 1,500 of the ¼-ton vehicles was considered. The Quartermaster proposed the purchase of 500 vehicles each from Bantam, Willys and Ford, although at that time the latter two firms had not yet produced a suitable pilot.

The proposed division of the order was not well received by the Infantry or Field Artillery branches, and concurrence from Cavalry was only conditional. The Quartermaster felt that including the other firms, even though they had not yet built a successful prototype, was worthwhile because this potentially could extend the field of development, and perhaps more notably align possible sources of mass production for the new type vehicle.

Ultimately, the decision was reached in late 1940 to procure 1,500 vehicles, to be delivered between March and 7 May 1941, each from American Bantam, Willys and Ford. These vehicles were designated models BRC, MA and GP respectively by their

In the early 1930s, America's strategic planners considered the motorcycle to be the future reconnaissance vehicle. However, some in the military wanted more armament and load-carrying capabilities. (National Archives)

manufacturers. The Ford designation GP was their product code "G" for government vehicle, and "P" for 80-inch wheelbase. While many enthusiasts today believe that the moniker jeep is derived from the Ford model designation, a congressional investigation into this in the 1940s found no evidence to support such a claim – nor in fact could any definitive source for the jeep name be found.

While the decision to include Ford and Willys in the production of the ¼-ton 4x4 was extraordinarily controversial and pitted the Quartermaster Corps against not only the using branches but also the War Department, this was not the only aspect of the ¼-ton truck procurement that saw the Quartermaster Corps at odds with the branches.

Of the 70 original Bantam-built vehicles, eight were four-wheel steer. The Cavalry especially appreciated the increased maneuverability offered by this feature, and pressed for further procurement of four-wheel steer ¼-ton trucks for additional testing. Presenting its case at a meeting of the Motor Vehicle Subcommittee 14 February 1941, Cavalry succeeded in stipulating that 100 of the newer vehicles being procured be equipped with four-wheel steering.

This stipulation was despite the Quartermaster's position, which was that four-wheel steer would increase maintenance, increase spare parts logistics and hinder production. The latter point was founded on the knowledge that driven steering axles were the critically short component not only in the production of the jeep – but all US tactical trucks. The four-wheel steer version of the vehicle would obviously require twice as many of these scarce components – not only for production but also for spares – as would the conventional two-wheel steer version.

On 11 April 1941 a directive from the Adjutant General was read to the Quartermaster Technical Committee directing that 50, rather than the 100 desired by Cavalry, four-wheel steer vehicles be procured for a sum not to exceed $60,000. The Committee recommended that these be allocated 36 to Cavalry, 6 to the Armored Force, three each to the Coast and Field Artillery and two the Quartermaster Corps.

Through negotiations, these vehicles were contracted from American Bantam at a bid price of $1,150 each. A short time later, the Quartermaster General was authorized to procure an identical quantity of four-wheel steer vehicles from the Ford Motor Company.

The 1,500 each purchased BRC, MA, and GP vehicles plus a further 2,958 GPs were subjected to field trials by the military. Each manufacturer's vehicle had strengths and weaknesses. The Army consequently solicited bids for an improved, standardized vehicle required to contain the best elements of each of the previous vehicles.

Bids were again solicited for the new, standardized vehicle. Willys was the low bidder with their new model, the MB. Many consider the MB to be the definitive military jeep.

Despite Willys being awarded the contract to produce the standardized jeep, Ford stayed in the quarter-ton truck game. Immediately before U.S. involvement in World War II, Willys faced financial and production capacity problems. Some in the Army believed Ford's solvency and enormous production capacity were the solution.

Accordingly, Ford was contracted to build functionally identical copies of the Willys MB. The Ford copy was given the model designation "GPW" – indicating Government vehicle, "P" – 80-inch wheelbase, "W" – Willys engine. Even the Willys "Go-Devil"

By 1937, Capt. Robert G. Howie and Master Sgt. M. Wiley had created a low-profile, lightweight machine-gun carrier. It paved the way for armed, four-wheel scout vehicles. Because the crew rode in the vehicle in the prone position, it was widely known as the "Howie Belly Flopper." Only a single example was built before attention turned to a more conventional motor vehicle. Many scholars consider the low-profile, four-wheel "Howie Belly Flopper" to be the direct predecessor of the jeep. (Robert Notman)

engine was duplicated by Ford. Many components of Ford-built jeeps are marked with the word Ford, or the company's script F logo. This is because vehicles sold to the government are covered under warranty, and Ford wanted to be sure that any parts returned to them as warranty claims were in fact Ford parts, rather than Willys.

The contract allowed some variation in design detail, as long as major assemblies interchanged. Whereas Willys used a heavy, welded grille that was labor-intensive to produce, Ford engineer Clarence Kramer designed a stamped steel grille that was faster, less expensive, and used less material to produce.

In early March 1942, Willys began using the Ford-designed stamped grille. In 1979, Chrysler (the corporate successor to Willys) was granted a trademark on the grille designed in Ford's studios.

Over the years, the standardized jeep's design evolved like most military vehicles. Manufacturer's names, once embossed on the vehicles, were eliminated. Windshield wipers changed from manually-operated to vacuum or electrically-operated. Brackets for fluid containers were added to the vehicle's rear, and spare-tire mounts were improved.

The MB and GPW continued to be used through the Korean War. Willys MC, known as the M38, was introduced during the Korean War. The M38 bore a striking resemblance to its predecessor. After only a short time, this vehicle was replaced by the Willys MD, also known as the M38A1.

The era of the classic jeep ended when the United States was fully involved in Vietnam and introduced the M151 series.

Ford GPW registration number 2058569, part of the first contract of 15,000 GPWs, is parked for a sense of scale next to the 1937 Experimental Carrier at Fort Benning, Georgia, in 1943. The unit markings on the jeep's bumper are "TIS-AD-I" and "AS-90."

Bantam

A column of early Bantam BRC-60 Reconnaissance Cars moves along a woodland trail in 1940. Two large grab handles on the body to the rear of the door are visible on the front vehicle. The windshield featured one large pane of glass. A single windshield wiper was mounted on the top of the windshield frame to the front of the driver. The grille that protected the radiator was formed of seven vertical metal tubes. The fronts of the hoods of these vehicles as viewed from above had a more flattened shape than that of the first Bantam Reconnaissance Car. They also featured more angular military-style fenders: compare the photo to the right. The headlights of these four BRC-60s rested in indentations on the top fronts of the fenders, and these lights had brush guards.

The prototype Bantam Reconnaissance Car, carrying a driver and two soldiers with Browning Automatic Rifles (BARs), precedes a Corbitt 50SD6 6-ton 6x6 cargo truck down a steep grade on 29 September 1940. Above the fender is the license plate, number 302 assigned to the Engineer Department at Holabird. The front of the hood is rounded and the prototype's windshield is of a single pane of glass in a light-duty frame with a thin transverse member at the bottom. In contrast, the windshield frame of the production BRC-60s had the thicker transverse bottom section seen in the photo to the left. The prototype Bantam Reconnaissance Car had somewhat complex, sculpted, civilian-style fenders, with distinctive cutouts to the bottoms of the service headlights.

The rear of the doors of the Bantam Reconnaissance Car have a characteristic scalloped or stepped shape. The simple canvas top, with an upper cover and a rear curtain, set the stage for the jeeps' canvas tops. The curved front fenders, however, were a luxury that would not feature on the jeeps of World War II.

A BRC-60 is outfitted with a .50-caliber machine gun at Aberdeen Proving Grounds in March 1941. The 70 vehicles built on the first contract were known as the Bantam Model 60, or Mark-II (Mk-2). Eight of these vehicles featured four-wheel steering, while the remaining 62 employed conventional two-wheel steering. The scalloped doorway of the prototype was replaced with a simpler opening. The elaborate fenders were also replaced with simple, flat versions. (Patton Museum)

The Bantam prototype at Fort Knox displays the graceful, curved fenders that soon gave way to the characteristic flat fenders. The Reconnaissance Car appears heavily burdened by the five men inside it. (Patton Museum)

Scout troops pose for a portrait with two Bantam Mark-II, Model 60 reconnaissance vehicles and a motorcycle. The Bantams and their successors would permanently alter the role of motorcycles in the U.S. military. (Military History Institute.)

The Bantam BRC-40 resembles the traditional military Jeep more than earlier models. The Reconnaissance Car was powered by a Continental four-cylinder engine with a 112-cubic-inch displacement. The Spicer 40 axles were coupled to the engine through a three-speed Warner T-84D transmission and a two-speed Spicer transfer case.

A Bantam BRC-60 demonstrates its speed, agility, and toughness by launching into the air with a towed 37mm anti-tank gun. Jeeps proved to be eminently suited to transporting the diminutive 37mm gun into action on battlefields from the Pacific to North Africa and Europe. (National Archives)

Soldiers row a pair of jeeps across a stream. The original specifications of the quarter-ton reconnaissance car specified a maximum weight of 1,300 pounds. Although the BRC-40 exceeded this amount by weighing 2,070 pounds, it was still light enough to be manhandled in extreme cases. (Army Motors)

The flat hood, fenders and slat grille were characteristic of World War II jeeps. The Bantam BRC-40 had all these features. (Military History Institute)

By 1941, a skidplate was added to the BRC-40 to protect the Spicer Model 18 transfer case. (Military History Institute)

The slab-sided body of the Bantam was festooned with grab handles. The handles were required specifications to allow man-handling of the vehicle. Interestingly, many people see the HMMWV as a descendant of the jeep. However, it's unlikely the latter could be manually lifted. (Military History Institute)

A BRC-40 is fitted with a 37mm anti-tank gun in 1941. The combination was designated T2E1. During testing, this combination caused the frame to crack. As long as the U.S. military fielded quarter-ton vehicles, efforts were made to give them tank-destroyer capabilities. Recoilless rifles, Davey Crocketts, and TOW systems became considerably more effective than early efforts following World War II. (Patton Museum)

An Army chaplain uses a BRC-40 as a temporary altar. An altar cloth is spread over the hood, and a crucifix is on the windshield frame. The glass panel of the windshield has been opened, and the frame has been folded forward. (Military History Institute)

A cargo net serves to move a Bantam BRC-40 from a transport ship during amphibious training maneuvers off the North Carolina coast. (Library of Congress)

A reconnaissance team includes four BRC-40s. Two vehicles are equipped with Browning .30-caliber machine guns on dash mounts. A third vehicle (second from left) is armed with a Browning Automatic Rifle (BAR). Bicycles are mounted on the right side of three Bantams. The jeep and motorcycle riders are wearing light-colored, soft, aviator-type helmets. The Dodge half-ton command and reconnaissance car on the right has a lucky horseshoe on its grille. (Jim Gilmore collection)

One experiment equipped the quarter-ton vehicles with four-wheel steering. Bantam introduced this feature on eight BRC-60 or Mk-2 jeeps from the first contract of 70 vehicles. Shortages of critical steering components, complexity to manufacture, and concerns for troop training and safety resulted in scrapping the four-wheel-drive-and-steer system. (Military History Institute)

Navy crewmen steady a BRC-40 during an on-deck transfer operation. For the relatively light jeep, simply driving its wheels onto cargo nets was an expeditious means of preparing the vehicle for loading. (Library of Congress)

Three G.I.s in a very muddy Bantam BRC-40 flirt with a carhop at a drive-in restaurant in Arkansas in September 1941. A civilian-type tire has been mounted on the left front wheel. The left windshield clamp is dangling over the fender, and the left arm of the windshield frame hangs loosely on the cowl, apparently broken off of the frame.

Bantam BRC-40 registration number W-2016951 drives across what appears to be an engineer bridge during Third Army maneuvers in Louisiana on 8 September 1941. There are markings for headquarters of a field artillery battalion on the bumper, but only the last digit of the battalion's number, 4, is visible. The windshield has been removed.

Bantam BRC-40

 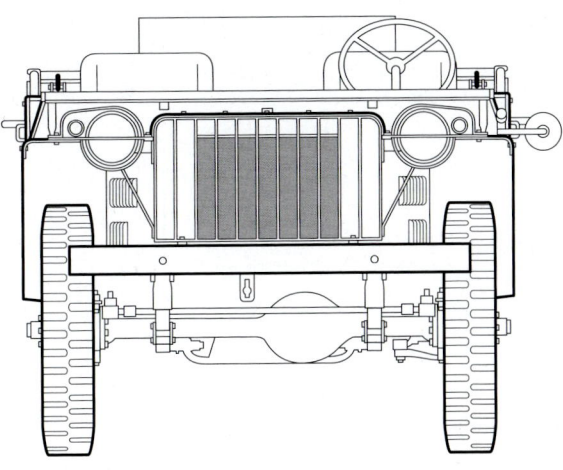

Ford GP

A driver and two G.I.s holding Browning Automatic Rifles (BARs) are riding in Ford GP number-one prototype, known as the Pygmy. Based on another photo showing the same vehicle and crew, it is likely that this photo was taken during a 5,000-mile continuous test run at Camp Holabird, Maryland, in November 1940. The placard on the grille has the number 2 on it.

The same front-seat crewmen shown in the preceding photo brace themselves as the first prototype Ford GP goes airborne during the 5,000-mile continuous testing at Camp Holabird in November 1940. The intricate grille soon would undergo simplification as the Ford jeep evolved.

In late 1940, the Budd Company of Philadelphia, Pennsylvania, built the body for a jeep prototype based on a Ford-designed chassis. A key feature was the position of the headlights, along with semicircular brush guards, on top of the fenders. The Budd-bodied pilot also had stepped door openings.

Soldiers ride in the Ford GP #1 prototype body during trials at Camp Holabird, Maryland, in November 1940. It had a flat hood and headlights recessed behind the grille. The Ford body had stepped edges at the rear of the doorways, a dogleg windshield hinge, and a welded slat grille. This feature carried over to the Ford GP. (Jim Gilmore collection)

A pilot Ford GP is parked at the River Rouge plant in November 1940. The front seats are bucket type, and safety belts are rigged across the door openings with the snaps attached to O-rings on the dashboard. The windshield was designed to open when the frame was in the upright position, using the hold-open arms on each side of the frame.

15

A Ford GP body is lowered onto a chassis. The man to the right operates a remote control for the overhead hoist. Protective material is wrapped around the fender.

Ford won a contract to build 1,500 reconnaissance trucks. The company assigned their model designation GP. This designation came straight from Ford's standard internal model designation system. In Ford's system, G designated government contract vehicle while P indicated an 80-inch wheelbase. (Army Motors)

Ford assembly-line workers put the final touches on GPs. Details of the interior of the hood are visible on the front GP, and behind the grille are the service headlights, below which are the blackout lamps. The horn is below and inboard of the left headlight.

Gen. Bonesteel (front) rides in a GP with Edsel Ford (rear). The 45-h.p. GP engine was based on the Ford 9N tractor engine driven through a three-speed unsynchronized Ford gearbox. The shift lever was mounted on the floor. (Army Motors)

A group of soldiers convene around a Ford GP. The registration number, W-2017951, is visible on the hood below the folded-down windshield. Above the steering column is a dome-shaped object, purpose unknown.

This pre-production pilot model has been sent to QMC for final testing, so it lacks a registration number. The bow-bracket wing nuts lack retainer chains on this model. (Military History Institute)

A civilian test driver puts a brand-new Ford GP through its paces prior to delivery to the U.S. Army in May 1941. Another GP stands by in the background. (Library of Congress)

Negotiating a steep gully during an exercise, this GP features distinctive gussets with cutouts on the bumper, a rearview mirror that has been reversed from the normal position, one rubber windshield rest on the centerline of the hood, and a safety strap next to the front passenger. (Library of Congress)

Jeeps at the Signal Corps Laboratories, Fort Monmouth, New Jersey, on 20 June 1941 are equipped for the Halstead Radio Traffic Control System. Patented in 1938, the system provided radio signaling for traffic-control systems, particularly directional signaling along specific traffic lanes. (US Army Communications and Electronics Command)

Three strong men lift the front end of a vehicle while a fourth soldier sits on the rear for counterbalance. The vehicle is equipped with early Firestone, "dogleg"-tread NDT tires. The soldier removing the lug nuts wears the shoulder patch of the 1st Armored Division. (Library of Congress)

The single GP acquired by the U.S. Marine Corps has had a second bow added. Front and rear bows attach to the same bracket and added webbing straps keep the front bow in place. The acute angle of the rear bow section is evinced at its lower end. (USMC)

The canvas top has been removed and the windshield lowered on the Marine GP. The front seats have been replaced with modified MB seats. The windshield latch is located at the lower left, and bolts secure the grab handles inside the body. (USMC)

In 1941 the U.S. Army contracted for 50 four-wheel-steering jeeps in order to gain improved maneuverability. This example, a Ford GP completed in September 1941, featured a delayed rear-wheel-steer action, which gave the vehicle improved agility in avoiding trees and other obstacles.

This mud-splattered Ford GP, registration number W-234111, is one of 50 GPs fitted with four-wheel steering under Quartermaster Corps (QMC) contract W-398-QM-10651. This example had two rubber windshield rests on the hood. Only the driver-side windshield panel was supplied with a top-mounted windshield wiper. On the top transverse member of the windshield frame were 10 snap fittings for attaching the front end of the canvas top. On the front vehicle, snap fittings for attaching a canvas door also are visible around the opening for the driver's door. (Library of Congress)

The driver of a Ford GP, U.S. Army registration number W-234099, and another G.I. gaze at something, apparently the tread of the left front tire. The registration number was painted in Blue Drab paint, which had lower visibility than white. A clear view is available of the front left wheel. This is a solid-disc wheel without vent slots. The wheel, mounted on five lugs, was 16 inches in diameter, with a size 6.00-16 tire with non-directional tread. All Ford GPWs would be issued with two-piece split combat rims with eight bolts securing the two halves together, and with vent slots. (Ordnance Museum)

Ford GP

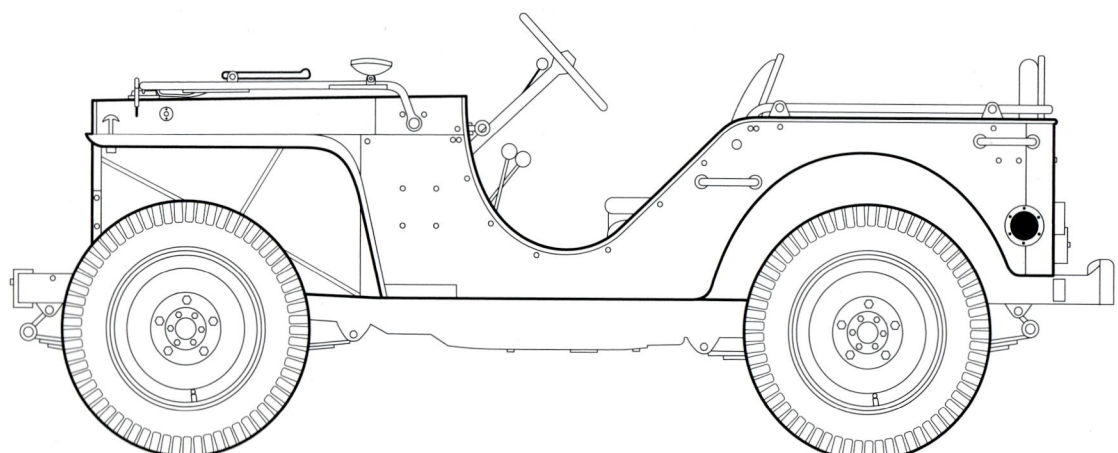
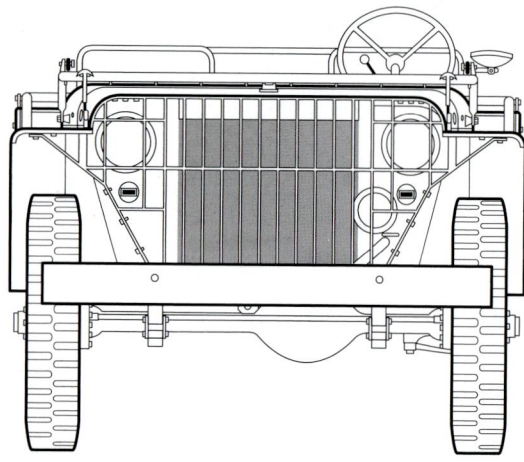

Willys Quad & MA

The Willys Quad was the firm's initial prototype attempt to capture the quarter-ton reconnaissance car market. The effort proved successful, although its fender and lighting arrangement were significantly modified on later models. (Ordnance Museum)

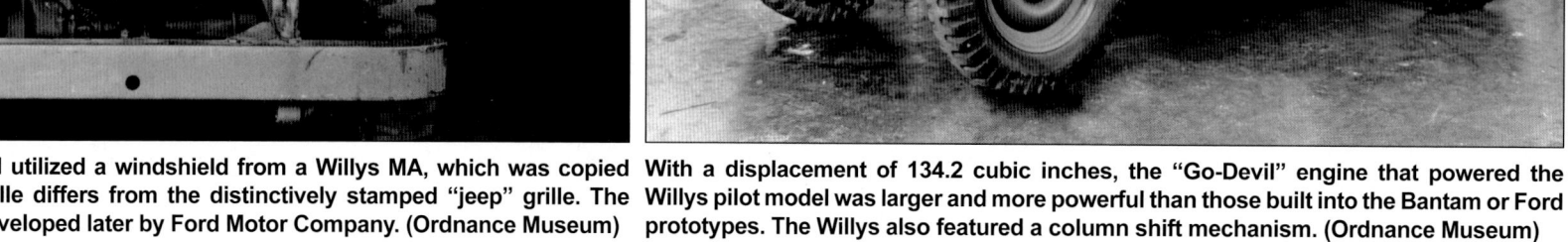

This Quad was rebuilt and utilized a windshield from a Willys MA, which was copied from the Ford GP. The grille differs from the distinctively stamped "jeep" grille. The stamped grille was also developed later by Ford Motor Company. (Ordnance Museum)

To fill a military contract for 1,500 field-trial vehicles, Willys engineers revamped the 1940 Quad, resulting in the Willys MA. A total of 1,553 MAs were produced, with the majority of them being shipped to the Soviets under Lend-Lease. (Military History Institute)

With a displacement of 134.2 cubic inches, the "Go-Devil" engine that powered the Willys pilot model was larger and more powerful than those built into the Bantam or Ford prototypes. The Willys also featured a column shift mechanism. (Ordnance Museum)

The name "WILLYS" was embossed on the front of MA hoods. On the MB version, both the embossed logo and fender-mounted headlights were eliminated. (Ordnance Museum)

Production of the MA ended in September 1941. Some vehicles remained at the factory and were scavenged for parts. However, this example remained in use until 1944. The dual-bow tarpaulin-support system is unique to this vehicle. (Ordnance Museum)

An MA negotiates the steps of the Willys-Overland administration building during a war-bond drive in September 1941. Three rubber windshield bumpers rather than one are on the hood, the result of a Modification Work Order (MWO). (Jim Gilmore collection)

An MA transports soldiers at The Desert Training Center. A tow rope is neatly wrapped around the bumper. A loose-fitting canvas cover encloses the windshield. The vehicle's name, "Cleo," is painted above the rear wheel well. (Library of Congress)

Gen. Dwight D. Eisenhower (left) and a South American officer pore over a map in a Willys MA. The tactical sign (AT-1-GP) on the grille is for an anti-tank unit Ike commanded in the war games. The fleur-de-lis is a tactical or unit sign. (Jim Gilmore collection)

A soldier briefs two foreign military officers about the MA's engine. The air hose is disconnected from the carburetor. Also visible are the distributor and dipstick/oil filler tube. (Jim Gilmore collection)

Santa commandeers an MA for Christmas in 1941. The jeep has been used in many roles beyond the imaginations of the original engineers. Such adaptations of the jeep have been prevalent since it was first fielded. (Military History Institute)

Standardized Quarter-ton 4x4

Willys MBs are loaded on railroad flatcars for long-distance shipment. They all have the so-called slat grilles that were a standard feature on the MB until early March 1942, when the stamped grille was introduced on the production lines. The grilles included a round brush guard to the front of the service headlights. Below the service headlights were blackout marker lamps. The front fender of the MBs had a single hole at the center for the manual starter crank for the engine.

A 37mm anti-tank gun towed by a Willys MB lifts off the ground after hitting a bump at speed. The Willys MB featured a grille welded from heavy-gauge slats on the first 25,808 examples. This jeep also has solid disk wheels. After the first 20,700 examples, MBs had combat rims. (Military History Institute)

Soldiers of the 161st Signal Photo Company power a table saw with a belt attached to the front wheel of an MB on blocks at Fort Benning, Georgia, around April 1942. (National Archives)

A soldier poses at a U.S. Army Engineer unit in England, where a Willys MB serves as a fire marshal vehicle. It tows a water-pump trailer and has a bell hanging from a bracket mounted on the front fender. The registration number identifies this MB as one built under contract W-398-QM-10757 in 1942. (U.S. Army Engineer School History Office)

Marines give a ride to a couple of Solomon Islanders in a slat-grille MB on Guadalcanal as a standard jeep follows. The windshield has been completely removed on this jeep and the one passing it. The slat-grille MB was superseded by what could be considered the "standard" MB. The standardized MB incorporated a stamped-steel grille developed by Ford. (USMC)

This slat-grille Willys MB has been fitted as a field ambulance. A tube frame supports a canvas top with red cross markings and storage for two extra stretchers. The outboard pole of the bottom stretcher is attached to hooks on the vertical frame, while the inboard pole is suspended with webbing straps. (Library of Congress)

A column of soldiers with the 11th Infantry's 81mm mortar section drive slat-grilled Willys MBs at Fort Custer, Michigan, in August 1942. The lead vehicle has hand-operated windshield wiper cranks and its windshield and hood are secured by hold-down clamps. (National Archives photo)

Soldiers hold M1 rifles as they pose for a portrait at a Signal Corps studio in a slat-grille MB. The brown cast to the olive-drab paint is a result of photographic chemistry. (National Archives)

The crew of this slat-grille Willys service the engine. The soldier at left holds an oil can. The smudge inside of the hood may indicate a sudden oil line rupture. A small star is sprayed over the hole for the manual starter crank on the bumper. (Patton Museum)

A Willys quarter-ton, four-by-four truck is parked during testing at Aberdeen Proving Grounds on 1 September 1943. Willys initially won the government contract to produce quarter-ton reconnaissance vehicles. Immediately before U.S. involvement in World War II, Willys faced financial and production problems. Some in the Army believed Ford Motor Company's solvency and production capacity were the solution. Consequently, Ford also produced the trucks based on the Willys model during World War II with the designation GPW.

The classic WWII jeep is typified by this Willys MB, registration number 20324814. The number indicates it was produced in 1943 under contract W-2529-QM-650. It has the stamped grille introduced to the MB after about 7 March 1942. (Ordnance Museum)

The MB features two louvers in the front wheel well. The grooves, brackets, and straps on the side of the body are for pioneer tools, the retainer chains for the bow and windshield hinge wing nuts. (Ordnance Museum)

The GPW, registration number 20380086, is tested at Aberdeen Proving Ground. It was manufactured in 1943. The bumper markings are repeated on both sides of the hood as "066 / AUTO TEST / ICT." The Ford GPW was, at a glance, identical to the MB, although the two models differ in fine details. (Military History Institute)

The exterior of the GPW was "busier" in appearance than its predecessor, the Ford GP. It featured additions such as the holders for a five-gallon gas can and pioneer tools, exterior-mounted bow brackets, and a fender-mounted blackout headlight. (Military History Institute)

The Quarter-Ton Goes To War

During WWII Willys-Overland motors had built 359,489 ¼-ton 4x4 trucks, and Ford 277,896 of the GPWs. Ostensibly identical, in fact there were slight variations between the two makes. Ford utilized a stamped steel grille throughout production, while the first 25,808 Willys MB used what is known as a "slat grille;" a welded assembly of heavy bar stock. The stamped grille was not only lighter weight, but also reportedly could be produced for about ⅓ the cost of the fabricated unit it replaced. After 12 June 1942 both makes used the Ford-designed lightweight stamped-steel grille.

The early models had "Willys" embossed in the rear body panel, and are known as "script" Jeeps. This practice was discontinued in July of 1942. Like the MB, earliest GPWs had the brand embossed in the familiar Ford script on the rear panel until July.

Ford built its own bodies at the Lincoln plant until the fall of 1943. At that time Ford began buying bodies from American Central, which was already supplying bodies to Willys. Ultimately, representatives of Ford, Willys, and the Ordnance Department created the composite body, incorporating the best of each maker's body. This body was used by both Ford and Willys beginning in the last months of 1943.

Regardless of maker, the jeep was enormously popular with troops and leaders. Jeeps were active in North Africa, in Europe, on aircraft flight decks and in Pacific jungles. Jeeps were configured for radio gear, armed with weapons, and bore stretchers. Large numbers of jeeps were also delivered to allied nations.

Students pose in a GPW from Headquarters Company of the 12th Armored Division. Jeeps were frequently involved in bond-raising drives and patriotic activities during WWII. This civilian introduction added to the vehicle's mystique. (Patton Museum)

During the First Army maneuvers in the Carolinas in the fall of 1941, a jeep is about to go airborne while driving at high speed over rough terrain. The rounded running board indicates that this was a Ford GP. (National Archives)

The foreground jeep, named "Cleveland," is a first-contract Ford GPW manufactured in early 1942. It is fitted with a radio set and a bazooka rack on the cowl. "C-12" is stenciled on the radio and windshield cover. A small "S" is painted on the cowl. (Patton Museum)

In 1942 the Field Artillery Board and the Ordnance Department developed a tandem A-frame hitch to connect two jeeps to fashion an expedient prime mover for the 105mm howitzer for airborne troops or for emergency use by the field artillery. (National Archives)

In May 1942 a convoy carrying Gen. Joseph Stilwell and his force passes along a highway between Burma and Imphal, India. At the front is a Ford GP. Marked on the window frame is the number 9 inside a circle, and "U.S. Army," with the Chinese equivalent below it. An insignia in the form of a shield is to the rear of the door. (National Archives)

A Bantam BRC-40 serves as a tow vehicle during testing of the 57mm Gun Carriage T1 at Aberdeen Proving Ground on 21 February 1942. The jeep was well suited for towing the smaller 37mm Antitank Gun M1, but a 57mm gun required a larger prime mover such as a half-track or Dodge weapons carrier for normal operational use. (National Archives)

At Fort Custer, Michigan, in August 1942, Willys MB registration number 2032431, is heavily armed with an early-type Browning .50-caliber M2 HB machine gun on a pedestal attached to the cowl and a BAR on a pedestal mount on the rear.

During the march of Lt. Gen. Joseph W. Stilwell's command from Burma to Imphal in May 1942, Maj. Gen. Franklin C. Siebert precedes a Ford GP on an engineer bridge. This was the first U.S. Army jeep to cross the Chinese-built bridge. (National Archives)

This slat-grille Willys MB was hauled ashore from a capsized landing craft at Fedâla, French Morocco, during the Operation Torch landings on 9 November 1942. The air cleaner and air-intake hose have been removed. (National Archives)

Two jeeps of the 531st Engineer Group with deep-fording kits, U.S. flags on the windshields, and 37mm antitank guns hitched are being prepared to move off the beach at Les Andalouses, Algeria, on 8 November 1942. (National Archives)

U.S. airmen tour the Great Pyramids at Gîza, Egypt, on 13 December 1942. The eight jeeps are painted a light color. All have stamped grilles. (National Archives)

Scores of jeeps are lined up at a motor park at Camp Polk, Louisiana, in 1942. The second vehicle in the row to the right is a Ford GPW, registration number 2055114, from a lot of vehicles that the Army accepted during the first few months of 1942. Parked to the rear of that GPW is another Ford GPW, 20109780, accepted by the Army during the period from April to October 1942. The Ford logo is stamped into the metal below the registration number. (National Archives)

This Ford GPW served as President Franklin D. Roosevelt's vehicle on an inspection tour of U.S. Forces in French Morocco during the Casablanca Conference in January 1943. The GPW's bumper bears markings for the 43rd Ordnance Battalion, I Armored Corps.

The same Ford GPW is viewed fro another angle, with FDR in the front passenger's seat and Fifth Army commander Lt. Gen. Mark W. Clark sitting in the middle in the rear seat. American flags were marked on each side of the hood.

A Mack NO 7.5-ton prime mover towers over a jeep at Camp Gruber, Oklahoma, in 1943. The vehicles represent the size range of U.S. wartime wheeled vehicles. The unit marking "3A-985F [national star] HQ-64" is painted on the jeep's front bumper. (Mack Museum)

A Studebaker US6 6x6 truck has just towed in a jeep suffering mechanical problems at the base of Patrol Service Unit (PATSU) 4-2 on Amchitka Island, Alaska Territory. This jeep has a hard enclosure, a passenger's door with a rhomboidal window, and a section of pipe for the front bumper. (National Archives)

On 18 February 1943, the day before the start of the Battle of Kasserine Pass, three occupants of a jeep look out for enemy activity as they transport a French commercial telephone switchboard, lashed to the hood, at al-Qaṣrîn (Kasserine), Tunisia. A five-gallon liquid container and a metal box are stowed on the front bumper. (National Archives)

Three ragged and haggard U.S. Army soldiers who were trapped behind German lines for three days during the Battle of Kasserine Pass have just arrived at an Army base in Tunisia on 26 February 1943. They are driving a Willys MB, registration number 2078475, which is armed with a pedestal-mounted Browning M1919 .30-caliber machine gun and is equipped with a radio. (National Archives)

On 1 March 1943, members of Marine anti-sabotage mobile units at the Puget Sound Navy Yard in Washington are ready for action in an IH Model M-2-4 1-ton truck, left, and three jeeps. All three jeeps are early Willys MBs with slat grilles. (Tracy White collection)

USMC jeep, registration number 40008, drives ashore from a landing craft during training maneuvers in Australia in April 1943. It was rare when the profile of the beach allowed the landing craft to lower its ramp directly onto the beach. (National Archives)

Jeeps and M4 tanks wait to load onto LSTs at Bizerte, Tunisia, before the Sicilian invasion in July 1943. A Higgins PT boat (right) undergoes repairs on a stand. (U.S. Navy)

In August 1943, the U.S. Army issued a requirement for a truck to transport pipeline equipment. The vehicle was developed at Fort Belvoir, Virginia, and was designed to operate on rough trails. It had racks for carrying up to eight sections of pipe and ample bracing was provided to stabilize the racks. The test vehicle shown here was Willys MB registration number 2061038. Marked on the front bumper are "AFS-E" and "Board 68." (US Army Corps of Engineers)

Sgt. Dow Flint examines a stack of two-ton blockbuster bombs from his 1942 Willys MB at the Eighth Air Force Service Command Depot at Sharnbrook, Bedfordshire, England on 7 July 1943. "PRUXC IV" is stenciled on the windshield frame. The headlights have been fitted with British blackout covers. The wheel cap is painted white. (National Archives)

Four members of the 417th Night Fighter Squadron pause for their portrait in Ford GPW registration number 20392434 at the Tafraoui (Ṭafrâwî) Air Base, about 17 miles south of Oran (Wahrân), Algeria, during World War II. A snap-on canvas curtain is on the door.

An ordnance heavy-maintenance company operates a jeep assembly line at Assembly Depot 0-640 in Tidworth, Wiltshire, in England on 8 September 1943. It was the only jeep-assembly facility in England. Partially assembled jeeps were delivered in crates, and finished jeeps left the depot every three minutes. (National Archives)

Assembly-line workers attach a windshield to a Willys MB at Tidworth on 8 September 1943. Bows lie inside the vehicles and towing pintles are on the rear seats as a man pushes a cart stacked with wheels farther down the assembly line. (National Archives)

The first step in assembling jeeps at the Tidworth depot was unpacking the crate containing the body/chassis assembly. The wheels are packed inside the body and secured with steel strapping. (National Archives)

Workers snap canvas onto the top of the jeep windshield frame at the Tidworth assembly line in England. The cover will then be pulled over the bow, already in place and ready to support the canvas top. The gasoline can holder, spare tire bracket, and rear axle assembly are visible. (National Archives)

A control jeep prepares to lead a B-24 at an airfield. The mustard-brown area between the star and the surround is a chemical-detecting paint. The paint changes colors when exposed to chemical attack. The canister on the fender is a decontamination cylinder. The U.S. Army Air Forces used jeeps to guide aircraft to takeoff positions and parking spots on busy, complicated airfields. These jeeps were called control jeeps, or "Follow Me" jeeps. They often had signs stating "Follow Me" on the rear of the vehicles. At forward airfields, the vehicles were painted Olive Drab. Elsewhere, control jeeps were painted yellow or checkerboard schemes for high visibility. They usually carried a radio set. (National Archives)

A soldier mans a .50-caliber machine gun on a pedestal mount at Eighth Air Force Station 167, Ridgewell, Essex, in England on 14 August 1943. The weapon platform was used for anti-aircraft defense. The "S" after the registration number indicates the vehicle passed a radio-interference suppression test. (National Archives)

A .30-caliber air-cooled Browning machine gun is mounted on an arm extending from a pedestal with a seat and safety belt for the gunner at Eighth Air Force Station 167 on 14 August 1943. The unusual anti-aircraft gun mount was possibly adapted from an aircraft mount. A ring sight is on the side of the arm, and the gunner has an elevating wheel. The gunner could use his legs to traverse the mount. Behind the gunner are two vertical equilibrator springs to counterbalance the weight of the gun. The driver's seat back and the passenger seat have been removed for gunner mobility. The X registration number indicates that this registration number is not the vehicle's original number. It is likely a former Lend-Lease machine transferred back to U.S. service. (National Archives)

A Ford GPW is put to work on a dock at Townsville, Australia, where Douglas A-20s are being unloaded from the escort carrier USS *Copahee* (CVE-12: not visible from this angle) during World War II. (National Archives)

Ordnance personnel install the windshield on Willys MB registration number 20329461 at the vehicle-assembly facility at Depot O-69 at Aintree, near Liverpool, England, on 7 October 1943. Partially disassembled jeeps were shipped from the United States to the depot, where they were reassembled. (National Archives)

A jeep performs as an ambulance in the Pacific Theater. The front stretcher holder, made from metal bars, is attached to the front bumper and the front fenders' rear. Unit markings are sprayed on canvas and affixed to the bumper. (Military History Institute)

Navy radiomen in a jeep marked "ACORN-9" are communicating by radio with personnel on the landing ship, tank (LST) in the background during a practice beach landing at Point Mugu, California. The radiomen were part of the Acorn Training detachment at Port Hueneme, California. (National Archives)

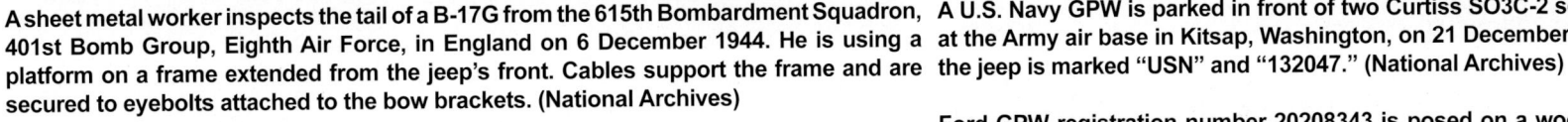

A sheet metal worker inspects the tail of a B-17G from the 615th Bombardment Squadron, 401st Bomb Group, Eighth Air Force, in England on 6 December 1944. He is using a platform on a frame extended from the jeep's front. Cables support the frame and are secured to eyebolts attached to the bow brackets. (National Archives)

Pvt. William J. Weinstock radios an aircraft while Pvt. Robert P. Wray sits behind the wheel in Kwajalein on 15 February 1944. Stenciled on the jeep is "94314-L." The prefix of 94- usually indicates a Navy vehicle. (National Archives)

A U.S. Navy GPW is parked in front of two Curtiss SO3C-2 scout/observation airplanes at the Army air base in Kitsap, Washington, on 21 December 1943. The front bumper of the jeep is marked "USN" and "132047." (National Archives)

Ford GPW registration number 20208343 is posed on a wooden bridge on the Burma Road for purposes of conveying the comparative size of the structure, on 17 March 1944. An M1 carbine is stowed in a scabbard that has been improvised from a canvas bag. (National Archives)

A GPW is parked on the USS *Lexington* (CV-16) flight deck in November 1943. The jeep was used as a flight deck tractor during operations in the Gilbert Islands. Unnecessary gear, such as the windshield, the bow, and its brackets, has been removed. A yellow chock was placed under the rear wheel to keep the vehicle from moving with deck pitches. (U.S. Navy)

Willys MB registration number 20306170 is loaded with radio equipment. On the near side is a case for Receiver Units, Medium Frequency, CCT 46076, and High Frequency, CCT 46077. On the far side are three sets, from front to rear: I.F. Transmitter CAY 52238, Rectifier Modulator CAY 20084, and H.E. Transmitter CAY 52239. (Mare Island Museum)

Radio equipment in a jeep in England on 24 March 1944 includes a transmitter-receiver (left) and an SCR-284 radio (right). This vehicle was assigned to a joint assault signal company for the impending invasion of Normandy. (National Archives)

A radio operator works in the rear of a joint assault signal company jeep, Willys MB registration number 446593 on 24 March 1944. This vehicle would coordinate communications for air-liaison, naval fire-control, and landing forces. (National Archives)

In a jeep photographed for the Shop Superintendent's Office, Mare Island Navy Yard, California, on 24 March 1944, an SCR-608 radio set is mounted in the rear. On the floor in the foreground is a Willys 12-volt generator, operated by the power takeoff, for supplying the required power to the radio. (Mare Island Museum)

MB/GPW General Data

Gross Weight	3,250 pounds
Net Weight	2,450 pounds
Payload	800 pounds
Length Overall	132.25 inches
Width Overall	55.5 inches
Height, top up	71.75 inches
Height, top down	52 inches
Track (center to center)	49 inches
Tire Size	6.00 - 16
Maximum Speed	65 miles per hour
Fuel Capacity	15 gallons
Fuel Type	68 octane gasoline
Range	300 miles
Maximum Towed Load	1,000 pounds
Electrical	6 volt negative
Transmission Speeds	3
Gear Ratio, High	Direct (1:1)
Gear Ratio, Low	2.665:1
Transfer Case Speeds	2
Gear Ratio, High	Direct (1:1)
Gear Ratio, Low	1.97:1
Axle Gear Ratio	4.88:1

Engine Data

Engine Model	442
Type	L-Head, 4-Cycle
Number of Cylinders	4
Cubic Inch Displacement	134
Bore	3.125 inches
Stroke	4.375 inches
Horsepower	54 @ 4,000 r.p.m
Torque	105 @ 2,000 r.p.m.

In preparation for an upcoming invasion, this jeep has been armed with a pair of flexible, aircraft-type Browning .30-caliber machine-guns at Finschhafen, Papua New Guinea, on 20 April 1944. The guns were mounted on a bracket on the right side of the dashboard. Tire chains are installed, and the service headlight is taped over. The hood has been removed and replaced with canvas and a deep-water air intake. (National Archives)

A Willys MB, left, and a Ford GPW are with Mine Detail Four at a South Pacific U.S. Navy mine depot. On the GPW windshield is stenciled "USN MINE DEPOT," along with a stylized U.S. Navy Bureau of Ordnance insignia: a flaming grenade with wings. The Bureau of Ordnance insignia on the windshield frame of the GPW is of a different design.

A group of Marines use muscle-power to extricate a Marine Corps ambulance jeep, commonly called a "Holden jeep," and its wounded patient from a river bed during the Cape Gloucester campaign on New Britain in 1944. (USMC)

Soldiers fill five-gallon water cans in a quarter-ton MBT trailer hitched to a jeep at the camp of the 115th Engineer Battalion, Cape Hoskins in New Britain on 30 June 1944. The blue-drab registration number suggests the vehicle was a Ford GPW from the 1943 production run. The jeep features a pedestal mount for a machine gun. (U.S. Army Engineer history office)

Navy personnel rest on the hood of a U.S. Navy jeep during a convoy pause. (National Archives)

On 14 May 1944, members of the 3rd Algerian Division of the French Army, serving with the Fifth Army, have lashed a goat to the lowered windshield of a jeep, part of the booty the division took at Coreno, Italy. Attached to the grille is a captured souvenir: a portrait of Adolf Hitler. (National Archives)

As forces of the 1st Canadian Infantry Division consolidate their hold on Frosinone, Italy, on 1 June 1944, one day after they captured the city, a jeep ambulance flying a red-cross flag stands by to the left. The vehicle was equipped with a stretcher rack extending to the rear of the vehicle. (National Archives)

An Army sergeant drives a jeep up the ramp of an LCT in England before the Normandy Invasion. The red-cross flag indicates medics will use it. A five-gallon can is tied to the grille, a leather scabbard lashed behind the front fender contains a rifle or carbine, and the rear end is piled with wooden crates and tarp-covered cargo. (National Archives)

Ambulance jeeps deliver Allied casualties to a beachhead in Normandy for transfer to landing craft that will take them to England for hospitalization. In the foreground is Willys MB registration number 20317220, equipped with a litter rack on the front end. Directly behind it is another jeep with litter racks on the front and the rear. (National Archives)

47

In preparation for the D-Day landings, a U.S. Army jeep backs onto the deck of an LCT in England. The pipe protruding from the hood on the passenger side is an air intake, part of the wading kit, which allowed vehicles to drive submerged for short distances when the landing craft was unable to discharge them directly on the beach. A wire cutter is mounted on the bumper. (National Archives)

The crew of *"I'll Get By,"* a B-17G of the 412th Bomber Squadron, 95th Bomber Group, rides a jeep to their aircraft in July 1944. The vehicle's spare tire is missing and probably deemed unnecessary for operation on the well-equipped and paved airfield. The bomber was shot down on 3 August 1944. Only three crewmen survived. (National Archives)

A 320th Field Artillery Battalion (Glider), 82nd Airborne Division jeep emerges from the cargo hold of a CG-4A Waco glider. Wooden gliders were capable of transporting a variety of loads, including one quarter-ton truck. The vehicle's 2/2 bridge weight classification plate indicates an approximate half-ton weight limitation.

49

1st Lt. Walter J. Lind of San Francisco elevates his leg on the cowl of a 1943 Willys MB. On the day before D-Day, he suffered a compound fracture of his right leg in a truck accident. His leg set in a cast, he landed in Normandy in the jeep on D-Day and supervised airfield construction in France. (National Archives)

A jeep assigned to the American Red Cross in Normandy delivers treats to troops in the field. "ARC" is painted on the bumper and on a placard. The grille is dented, and a small American flag decal is affixed on the windshield. (Don F. Pratt Museum)

A yellow Navy jeep in "Beachmaster" markings guides a C-46 Commando into place at N.A.S. Port Lyautey, Morocco, in 1944. Delivered in Army Olive Drab or Marine Corps green, Navy jeeps were repainted yellow or gray in the field or at depots. (U.S. Navy)

A U.S. Navy jeep is painted overall in a yellow high-visibility paint scheme in accordance with its role as a guide vehicle at an airfield during World War II. The USN registration number, 6338227-S, and the recognition star inside a circle, are painted in black. A yellow fire extinguisher is mounted on the rear of the fender.

A jeep travels through a French city while refugees return shortly after the liberation. A crate is strapped to the hood, a small star is painted at the center of the bumper, and the headlight lenses are sprayed with Olive Drab paint. (National Archives)

Maj. Gen. Maxwell Taylor rides in a jeep in Holland, possibly during Operation Market Garden in September 1944. His two-star placard and a roll of camouflage netting are secured to the bumper. (Don F. Pratt Museum)

Troops of the 327th Glider Infantry Regiment of the 101st Airborne Division back a jeep into a Waco glider before the Holland assault. (Don F. Pratt Museum)

A trooper examines a jeep from the 321st Glider Field Artillery Battalion of the 101st Airborne Division in Normandy. The vehicle's right and spare tires are burned. A German jerrycan is stored in the rack. "PRESTONE 44" was painted on the hood to signify the vehicle had been serviced with antifreeze in 1944. (Don F. Pratt Museum)

Members of the U.S. Army's 96th Signal Battalion have bundled their jeep in a tarpaulin, forming a makeshift vessel, to float it across the Mogaung River to the town of Kamaing, Burma, on 20 June 1944. (National Archives)

In a settlement on the Burma Road in 1944, Captain John H. Lattin, a convoy commander in the driver's seat of a Ford GPW, registration number 20208220, signals the drivers behind him to move out. On the windshield are a U.S. flag; a Chinese character signifying China's Expeditionary Force; and the insignia of Y-Force Operations Staff, Y-Force being the U.S. designation for Chinese forces that fought in Burma in World War II. (National Archives)

Ford GPW registration number 20208220 served in the CBI Theater in 1944. The registration number is in the factory-applied blue drab color.

Two jeeps are transporting a number of general officers and their aides on a tour of inspection of Japanese caves and fortifications on Biak, Dutch New Guinea (now part of the Indonesian province of Papua), on 29 June 1944. Their visit took place just a week after U.S. forces had broken through the Japanese defenses on 22 June, largely bringing to an end the battle for Biak island, which had been raging since the Americans landed there on 27 May 1944. No markings are visible on the jeeps. The bumper on the front vehicle is that of a Ford GPW, with three holes. (National Archives)

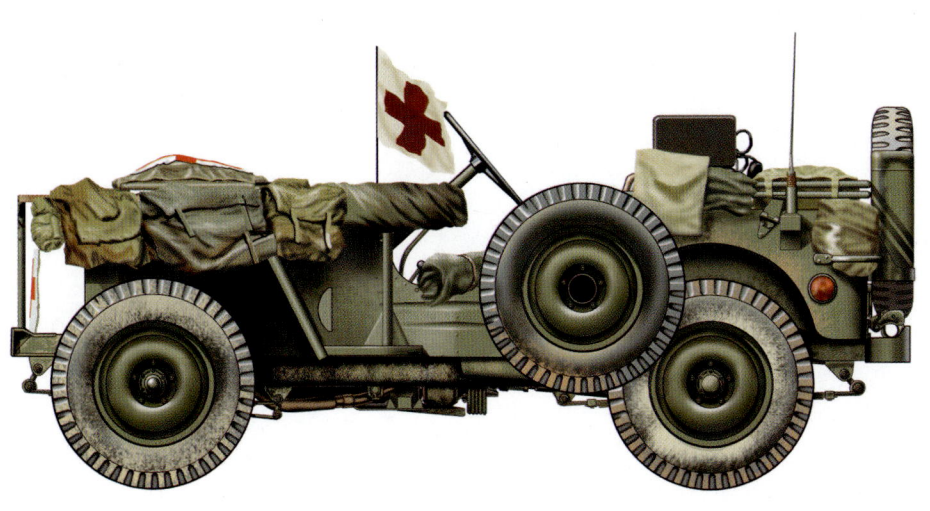

Able to negotiate rough ground and off-road conditions, jeeps often served as battlefield ambulances in WWII. This example served a 2nd Armored Division unit in the final months of the war in Europe. It had a rack for a single stretcher on the right side of the vehicle's front end. It had an extra spare tire next to the driver and a radio set in the rear.

Various Red Cross flags, placards, and emblems are displayed on a radio-equipped ambulance jeep from the 2nd Armored Division in Europe in 1944 or 1945. The front stretcher rack is fabricated from angle irons with large gussets at the bumper. The spare tire placement by the driver is unusual. (Patton Museum)

An amphibious variant of the jeep was part of the early proposal. This came to fruition in the form of the Ford-built GPA (GP-amphibious), jointly designed by Ford and Sparkman-Stephens. (Patton Museum).

Although used in Sicily, these GPAs are parked in a depot in England in preparation for the Normandy invasion. Too small to carry much cargo and unwieldy off-road, unlike its larger sibling the DUKW, the GPA was not considered a success. (National Archives)

A jeep passes a German Pz.Kpfw. IV tank knocked out by a direct hit by an artillery shell in the Pontedura area in Italy on 18 July 1944. On the bumper are very faint unit markings, "91-916F," referring to the 916th Field Artillery Battalion, 91st Infantry Division. A wire cutter is installed on the front end, and a disc with a heart-shaped object below it is affixed to the grille next to the left headlight. (National Archives)

Japanese-American members of a Nisei unit ride in a Willys MB through recently captured Leghorn (Livorno), Italy, on 19 July 1944. The placard on the grille reads "ICU," and the unit markings on the bumper read "5A-X" and "C." (National Archives)

A medical team from the 100th Infantry Battalion ride on their ambulance jeep near the end of World War II. The 100th Infantry Battalion was one of two Japanese-American, or Nisei, combat units in the U.S. Army during the war, the other being the 442nd Regimental Combat Team. Serving with the 34th Infantry Division, the 100th saw combat from Anzio to Cassino, Italy, and beyond. The battalion was awarded the Distinguished Unit Citation. (National Archives)

Two jeeps are part of a U.S. Army column passing through Mayenne, France, on 6 August 1944. The closer vehicle is pulling a trailer. The number 90 on the bumper probably indicates this vehicle was in a unit of the 90th Infantry Division.

Mechanics, three of whom are holding welding equipment and a large drill, pose next to a jeep. One may surmise that they have just completed installing the pedestal mount with a Browning .30-caliber machine gun to the front of the right door.

Private Albert C. Monferatto, wearing the armband of the U.S. Army Counterintelligence Corps, relaxes with his pipe behind the wheel of a jeep nicknamed "PANZERDOWN" at St.-Jean-de-Daye, France, on 22 July 1944. A pair of baby boots is hanging from the grab handle for good luck. (National Archives)

A soldier regards the remains of Willys MB registration number S-20351412 on 4 August 1944. The jeep detonated a mine near St.-Sever-Calvados, severing the vehicle in half. The explosion blew the front right wheel off. (National Archives)

Advancing G.I.s pause to watch a German ammunition dump that is on fire in France on 24 August 1944. The jeep to the left is a Willys MB, registration number S-20326520, while the one to the front of it is a Ford GPW, S-20420491. (National Archives)

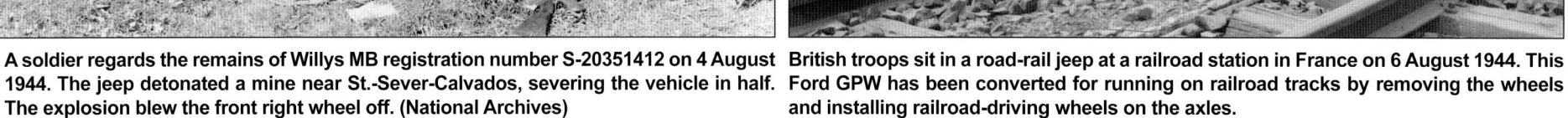

British troops sit in a road-rail jeep at a railroad station in France on 6 August 1944. This Ford GPW has been converted for running on railroad tracks by removing the wheels and installing railroad-driving wheels on the axles.

Mechanics of the 3507th Ordnance Medium Automotive Maintenance Repair Field Shop replace the damaged transmission of Willys MB registration number 20482153-S at Valconces, France, on 25 August 1944. (National Archives)

In the front passenger seat of his personal Willys MB, Lieutenant General Mark Clark, commander of the U.S. Fifth Army, crosses an engineer bridge over the Arno River in Florence, Italy, on 30 August 1944. At the wheel is Master Sgt. Robert Holden, General Clark's personal bodyguard. A plaque with the Fifth Army's insignia adorns the left front of the vehicle and four extra horns are arrayed in front of the grille. (National Archives)

A French civilian shakes his fist at two German prisoners of war on the hood of a jeep on 31 August 1944. The men were captured in Savigny, France. (National Archives)

Soldiers stop to confer next to a Ford GPW with markings for Recon Company, 67th Armored Regiment, 2nd Armored Division, near Barenton, France, in August 1944. A Thompson submachine gun is in a scabbard to the front of the driver. (National Archives)

This Willys MB was the first jeep to cross the German border at Roetgen, on 10 September 1944. At the wheel is a G.I., and his passenger is a member of the Belgian resistance. A flexible fuel-can nozzle is stuck in the grab handle on the side of the body. (National Archives)

Some of the 1,500 jeeps assembled at Ordnance Depot O-62, La Cambe, Normandy, are seen on 16 September 1944. Second from right in the front row is an early slat-grille Willys MB. The two jeeps to the front left are later MBs. (National Archives)

The nearest of two jeeps seen at Eloyes, France, on 24 September 1944 has a bicycle secured to the rear end and an antenna base unit on a bracket on the side of the cowl. To the rear are troops of the 141st Infantry, 36th Infantry Division. (National Archives)

The Ordnance Department developed a portable arc-welding kit for jeeps in 1943. It fit next to the driver's seat and included a PTO-driven General Electric 200-amp, 30-volt generator; a governor; a modified fuel tank; an electrode; and cables. (National Archives)

The portable arc-welding kit as installed in Ford GPW registration number 20380215 is seen from a higher angle in a 2 September 1944 photo. A data plate for the kit is affixed to the body above the wheel well. (National Archives)

The driver of a jeep stops to check something alongside the vehicle at the German frontier in the fall of 1944. Of interest are the metal canister – not a liquid container – strapped to the right side of the cowl, and the double five-gallon liquid containers, on tandem holders, to the left of the spare tire. (National Archives)

Soldiers of the Fifth Army push a jeep mired in deep mud on a mountainside in the Gabbiano area of Italy on 10 October 1944. The chains on the tires of the nearest vehicle, a slat-grille Willys MB, appear to be having minimal positive effect on the vehicle's traction in these conditions. (National Archives)

On Leyte in the Philippines on 21 October 1944, members of the 34th Infantry Regiment inspect a Ford GP that the Japanese had captured during their invasion of that island in early 1942. (National Archives)

A jeep of the 16th Signal Battalion, Sixth Army, waits to board LST-697 at Pie Beach, Hollandia, Dutch New Guinea, on 13 October 1944. Stenciled above the rear wheel is 4021-E. Tire chains are mounted for better traction on sand and mud. (National Archives)

G.I.s listen to a broadcast of the 8 October 1944 World Series game between the St. Louis Browns and the St. Louis Cardinals. The wire cutter on the front of the Ford GPW is well buttressed with a single upper brace and a V-shaped lower brace. A Browning M1919 .30-caliber machine gun is mounted in the right side of the cowl. (National Archives)

Maj. Gen. John Millikin, U.S. 3rd Corps commander, is the front passenger in a jeep being towed on a flooded street in Pont-à-Mousson, France, on 9 November 1944. The nearby Moselle River was at its highest flood stage in some 30 years. (National Archives)

Members of a U.S. Army engineer battalion have placed a wounded comrade on the hood of a GPW for evacuation. This GPW has dissimilar tire treads, rolled up door curtains on the canvas top, and in front of the grille an unusual water container with an embossed letter W and a reel of communications wire. (National Archives)

A long-range, large-caliber German shell tore this jeep to pieces; it was photographed around Sarrebourg, France, on 24 November 1944. The entire vehicle was riddled with shrapnel. Even the shovel stored on the side of the body was cut in half, with the handle dangling from its retainer strap. (National Archives)

At the base of the 79th Ordnance Battalion at Verdun, France, on 29 November, wrecked vehicles have been deposited at this collecting point and are awaiting salvaging. Many of the vehicles, including in the foreground, are jeeps. (National Archives)

61

Soldiers balance a surgeon's jeep in Belgium. A pole holds a red medical cross flag behind the spare tire. The spare tire is positioned unusually in front of the grille. (Don F. Pratt Museum)

Lt. Gen. George Patton rides in a 1944 Willys MB in Belgium. The vehicle carries a pedestal-mounted .30-caliber Browning machine gun as well as markers signifying a Third Army lieutenant-general's vehicle. (Don F. Pratt Museum)

A radio-equipped jeep of the 30th Division drives down a snowy street in Malmedy, Belgium, during the winter of 1944-1945. The wire cutter is significantly bowed. A spare tire is mounted behind the driver on the vehicle's side. (Military History Institute)

A convoy moves in the First Army sector near Werbomont, Belgium in the winter of 1944-1945. Factory-supplied soft tops were replaced with simple tarps for protection from the elements. The rear jeep has tire chains. (Military History Institute)

The driver of a jeep assigned to a tank-destroyer battalion of the 90th Infantry Division blows on a tuba during a break on a street in Sankt Barbara, Germany, on 13 December 1944. A rack with Jerry cans is on the rear of the jeep. (National Archives)

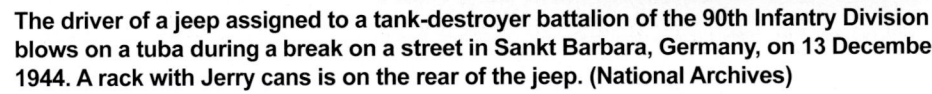

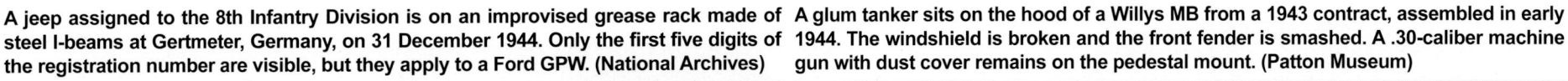

Major General Joseph "Lightning Joe" Collins, commander of U.S. VII Corps, is riding in a Willys MB near Düren, Germany, on 10 December 1944. The jeep has a siren on the fender and heavy-duty wire cutter. (National Archives)

A jeep assigned to the 8th Infantry Division is on an improvised grease rack made of steel I-beams at Gertmeter, Germany, on 31 December 1944. Only the first five digits of the registration number are visible, but they apply to a Ford GPW. (National Archives)

A glum tanker sits on the hood of a Willys MB from a 1943 contract, assembled in early 1944. The windshield is broken and the front fender is smashed. A .30-caliber machine gun with dust cover remains on the pedestal mount. (Patton Museum)

A U.S. Army lineman at the top of a telephone pole is stringing telephone lines while his jeep is parked below. A bracket on the rear of the jeep supports a reel of telephone cable. An extra tarp has been lashed over the standard canvas top to provide extra protection from the weather on the sides of the vehicle. (National Archives)

Supreme Allied Commander, Southeast Asia, Lord Louis Mountbatten, pokes his head out of a road-rail jeep on the railroad between Mogaung and Sahmaw, Burma, in late 1944. The grille has been damaged, and a wooden beam has been lashed to the bumper for extra protection to the front end. (National Archives)

Ordnance personnel of the U.S. Seventh Army in the Wiesviller area of France developed this rocket-launcher mount for a jeep. It included 12 4.5-inch launcher tubes, arranged six over six, on a stand and a partially enclosed cab to protect the driver from the blast from the rockets taking off. In this photo dated 27 December 1944, the launcher tubes are at maximum elevation and the G.I. inside the cab is operating an elevation hand crank. (Chris Benedict collection)

Few jeeps were equipped with rocket launchers. Anti-aircraft launchers had twelve 4.5" tubes. A metal enclosure protected the interior from the back-blast during firing. (Patton Museum)

In January 1945 the U.S. Army Services of Supply (SOS) sent their first all-SOS convoy from Burma to China over the Tengchung Cutoff. Here, Chinese civilians cheer as a jeep rolls through Tengchung (currently Téngchōng) on 17 January. (National Archives)

The same SOS convoy over the Tengchung Cutoff arrives in Tengchung (Téngchōng) in eastern Yúnnán Province. The lead vehicle has the three-hole front bumper of the Ford GPW. Tire chains are installed on the tires. (National Archives)

Twin bazookas are mounted on the machine-gun pedestal of a jeep of the 60th Infantry Regiment, 9th Infantry Division, in the European Theater on 12 January 1945. The jeep also had thin armor plate with a vision slot for the driver. (National Archives)

Crew members of an M8 Armored Car help medics push an ambulance jeep over a rutted stretch of trail outside of Asch, Luxembourg, on 26 January 1945. Two wounded German soldiers lie on stretchers on the jeep, and racks for two more stretchers are on the front of the vehicle. Markings for the 53rd Infantry, 4th Armored Division, are on the bumper; a red cross on a white field is painted on the grille; and the nickname "MY DOPY II" is marked above the rear wheel well. (National Archives)

Jeeps, like many other tactical vehicles, were sometimes whitewashed as a means of camouflage during the winter. The crew of this jeep has placed a spare tire between the front bumper and grille where it rests nicely on the frame rails with no straps required.

Several jeeps pass a column of trucks on a narrow road near Wallerode, Belgium, on 30 January 1945. The nearest jeep bears markings on its bumperettes for Company C, 307th Airborne Engineer Battalion, 82nd Airborne Division. A slightly out-of-level patch is noticeable on the upper right of the canvas top of this vehicle. (National Archives)

67

Filipino civilians help push a Willys MB, tires spinning, off the beach during a landing operation on Luzon in early 1945. What appears to be the cabinet for a large radio set is installed transversely to the rear of the front seats. (National Archives)

This jeep was armed with a .50-caliber machine gun on a mount installed on the top of the cowl. Unlike the pedestal-mounted machine guns found on some jeeps, this weapon was of little use in antiaircraft defense; it was more for applying firepower to the front.

A U.S. Marine Corps jeep is armed with a .30-caliber machine gun on a pedestal mount. The markings "USMC" and the Marine Corps registration number are painted in yellow on each side of the hood. Tire chains give better traction on sand and soft ground.

A driver in a jeep with a pedestal-mounted .30-caliber machine gun on the right side and a recognition star on the windshield cover watches as a column of M4 Medium Tanks drives past shell-pocked buildings in Krefeld, Germany, in early March 1945.

Three German prisoners of war sit on the hood of a jeep of the 8th Armored Division, U.S. Ninth Army, in Kamp-Lintfort, Germany, on 6 March 1945. Crude, battered, sheet-metal mudguards have been installed on the fronts of the fenders. (National Archives)

While members of Task Force Byrne pause at Sevelen, Germany, on 5 March 1945, a Willys MB with improvised mudguards on the fenders and markings for the 134th Infantry Regiment, 35th Infantry Division, is parked to the left. (National Archives)

A small dog is on the baggage in the rear of a jeep preceding two M8 armored cars in Remagen, Germany, on 10 March 1945. In front of the passenger is what appears to be a .30-caliber machine gun with a dust cover, in a vertical position. (National Archives)

A jeep pulls rolls of bituminous strips for surfacing a Ninth Air Force airstrip in Germany. Aviation engineers of the IX Engineer Command for a Ninth Air Force airfield fabricated these bituminous strips. The jeep drives over a surface fabricated from Marsden matting, perforated steel strips used to rapidly build temporary airstrips. Engineers use a strip of matting as a sled for the bituminous rolls. (National Archives)

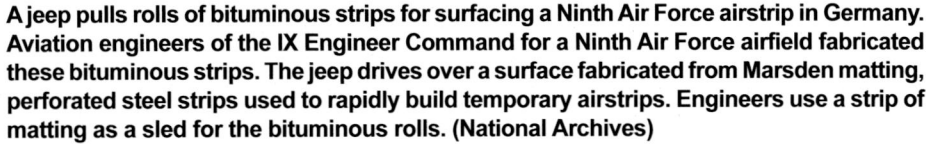

A German shepherd "takes five" on the driver's seat of a jeep, while a tech sergeant keeps his hands warm. The Willys MB was produced in early 1944. This jeep has an encircled, larger-than-usual star on the hood. The webbing straps for the pioneer tools are caked with mud. (Patton Museum)

A boy runs past several jeeps stopped in a war-wracked town in the Rhine River valley in early 1945. The jeep to the right has two reels of communications cable on a rack at the rear of the vehicle, as well as a German jerrycan in the fuel can rack. The forward jeep is hitched to a quarter-ton trailer. The canvas top of the jeep has been detached from the top of the windshield, folded, and laid down over the gear stowed in the rear of the vehicle. (National Archives)

Medics remove a seriously wounded soldier from a jeep to a waiting stretcher. The radio-equipped vehicle is a stock jeep rather than a field ambulance, which would be fitted with stretcher racks. (Patton Museum)

Donald Jensen, a liaison driver with the 2nd Cavalry Group, scrubs down his muddy jeep in a tributary of the Rhine River at Mayen, Germany on 12 March 1945. The windshield has a field modification with a new frame and bent metal plate. A stock windshield with the hinges cut off was reattached. (National Archives)

At the front of a column of 90mm Gun Motor Carriages M36 of the 301st Tank Destroyer Battalion, 3rd Infantry Division, Seventh Army, during the battalion's advance on the Bad Dürkheim-Ludwigshafen Highway in Germany on 23 March 1945 is a Ford GPW with markings for Company B of the 301st. To the right is a jeep with markings for Headquarters, 305th Combat Engineer Battalion, 80th Infantry Division. This jeep has a stowage rack on the rear end as a field modification, and a spare and a wire cutter on the front of the vehicle. (National Archives)

A column of jeeps carrying members of the 63rd Infantry Division, U.S. Seventh Army, pauses on a street in St. Ingbert, Germany, on 21 March 1945. A rifle bracket is mounted on the bottom of the windshield frame of the first jeep, and an M1 carbine with a magazine pouch on the stock is lying on a folded tarpaulin to the rear of the rifle bracket. On the bumper of a jeep in the middle background are markings for the 253rd Infantry Regiment of the 63rd Infantry Division. (National Archives)

These Marines in a Willys MB in mid-March 1945 had been transporting ammunition by jeep to the front lines on Iwo Jima for three weeks. A pioneer tool rack salvaged from a truck is mounted on the side. (National Archives)

The driver of a Ford GPW carrying Admiral Arthur D. Struble and Lt. Gen. Robert L. Eichelberger, commanding general of the U.S. Eighth Army, has stopped to ask directions from an MP in Iloilo City, Panay, Philippine Islands, on 30 March 1945. (National Archives)

A native guide on the left rear of a Marine jeep helps a team locate Japanese positions during a battle in the Pacific Theater. On the windshield frame is the Unit Numerical Identification System symbol for the 1st Marine Division. (National Archives)

A jeep with a two-tiered stretcher rack made from pipe fittings is about to depart with a load of casualties bound for an aid station on Okinawa on 19 April 1945. A small red-cross insignia is visible on the windshield frame. (National Archives)

Pfc. Charles J. Duffley of the 1st Battalion, 21st Marines poses for a portrait beside a trailer of flamethrowers in Iwo Jima. In addition to the spade and axe, a mattock pick is stuck through a grab handle. (National Archives)

Corpsmen transport wounded Marines on a Holden ambulance jeep in Iwo Jima. Several casualties are on stretchers, while a wounded man sits on the hood. The jeep features camouflage paint and a storage box in the passenger door. (National Archives)

A Marine jeep ambulance speeds several wounded men to a field hospital on Okinawa on 13 May 1945. The corpsman hanging on to the rear of the stretcher frame holds a plasma bottle for the wounded man on the bottom stretcher. The vehicle features a storage bin door on the vehicle's side and a spare tire mount on the hood. A light-colored capital "I" within a circle is marked behind the fender. (National Archives)

A Marine jeep leads a line of International Harvester M-2-4 one-ton rocket trucks *en route* to the combat line at Hill 382 on Iwo Jima in 1945. The jeep, with its spare tire stowed on the hood, pulls a camouflaged trailer. The vehicles are assigned to one of the provisional rocket detachments. Each of the rocket trucks could fire 4.5-inch rockets in ripple salvo of 36. Two jeep ambulances are among the parked vehicles. (USMC)

Members of the 3rd Armored Division, U.S. First Army, relax and soak up some welcome sunshine in Geselwerder, Germany, on 9 April 1945. The nearest jeep has a pedestal-mounted .30-caliber machine gun on the right side of the cowl. (National Archives)

Exhausted members of a machine-gun crew of the 102nd Infantry Division, U.S. Ninth Army, have fallen asleep in a jeep during a halt in Möckern-Erxleben, Germany, on 15 April 1945. This is Willys MB registration number 2074527. (National Archives)

A German prisoner of war poses next to a jeep at Karlsruhe, Germany. The enclosure, which has been made to fit under the bows, appears, on close inspection, to have been constructed of ¾-inch plywood.

The U.S. Marine Corps used specially modified jeeps as ambulances. Known as the "Holden jeep" the vehicle has yellow stencils on the hood and body. A spare tire is stored on the hood, and the canvas top includes side curtains.

Members of the 327th Glider Infantry Regiment, 101st Airborne Division, tour Berchtesgaden, Bavaria. Elements of the regiment assisted in the capture the Eagle's Nest, Hitler's retreat, in Berchtesgaden on 4 and 5 May 1945. (National Archives)

After several years of hard fighting during the war in Europe, troopers of the 327th Glider Infantry Regiment can sightsee in the Bavarian Alps at Berchtesgaden. (National Archives)

In the spring of 1945, Czechoslovak citizens greet a U.S. Army column passing through their city. In the foreground is a Willys MB with "Gracie" painted on the windshield frame and markings for the 38th Field Artillery Battalion, 2nd Infantry Division. (National Archives)

Photographed in the Czechoslovak town of Černý Potok (called "Schwarzbach" during the German occupation), in May 1945, Willys MB registration number 20642451 has a stowage rack on the rear with angle irons around the edges, vertical slats on the sides, and horizontal slats on the rear. (National Archives)

Chaplain John T. Fournier (left) and his driver enter a jeep outside a chapel in Europe during World War II. Chaplains provided spiritual counsel to troops throughout the front. The agile jeep was ideally suited to transport chaplains and the moderate amount of gear they carried. The registration number, which has been painted in a careless pattern, identifies the Willys MB from the 1944 production run. (National Archives)

Two armored jeeps pass an abandoned German Jagdtiger tank hunter. The lead jeep has a placard signifying that it is the vehicle of a brigadier general, while the second jeep bears two stars of a major general. Both vehicles have armored plates over the windshield assemblies, with two vision slots, and wire cutters. The second jeep has front fender extensions. (Patton Museum)

A storage mount has been installed on the rear of this jeep and an extra spare tire is stowed on the front end.

Personnel handle supplies in a trailer hitched to a Willys MB attached to the Photo Section of the 17th Tactical Reconnaissance Squadron on Luzon in the Philippines in 1945. Marked on the windshield frame is "14 PHOTO 17R." The right side of the bumper is twisted. (US Air Force Academy)

Around the summer of 1945, a member of a signals battalion is at the wheel of a railroad jeep. The vehicle is a Ford GPW, as indicated by the hole in the bumper aligned with the left main chassis frame member. The spotlight is improvised from a civilian-type headlight and is on a pedestal that is mounted to the cowl. (National Archives)

A member of the 17th Tactical Reconnaissance Squadron performs routine maintenance on a Ford GPW at a base on Luzon in 1945. (US Air Force Academy)

A U.S. Army private paints "OFFICIAL PHOTOGRAPHER" on the windshield frame of Willys MB registration number 20322386 at Camp Miami, Châlons, France, on 26 June 1945. Below the grille is a Willys-type tubular cross-member. (National Archives)

An A-frame boom hoists a radio-equipped Willys MB-NOM-12 from a DUKW amphibious truck on Tinian on 25 July 1945. "NOM" referred to Navy contract for Marine Corps, and the number 12 referred to the vehicle's 12-volt electrical system. (USMC)

79

On 2 September 1945, the date of the formal Japanese surrender on the USS *Missouri* in Tokyo Bay, a curious crowd has gathered around the first jeep of the 11th Airborne Division to arrive in Tokyo. The registration number, 20538249, identifies this vehicle as a Ford GPW. (National Archives)